This Book Belongs to:

_____

_____

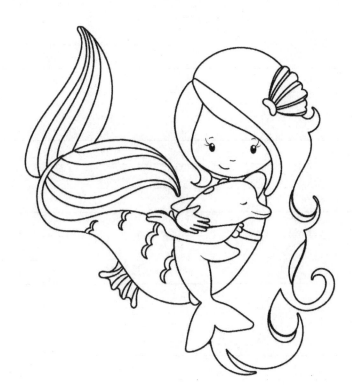

Dream Big
little Mermaid

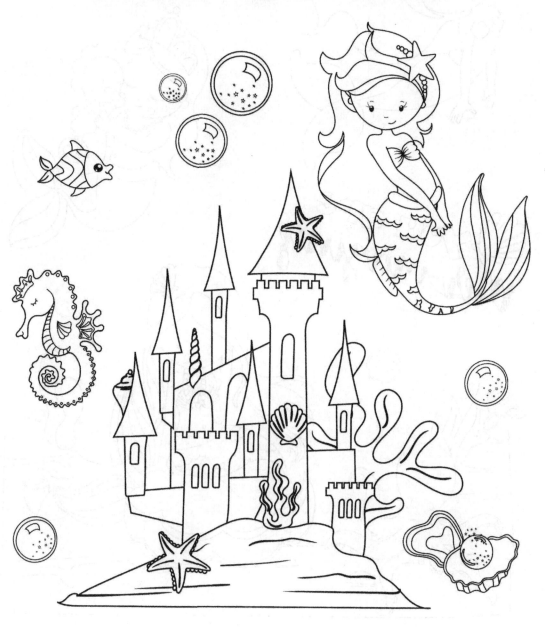

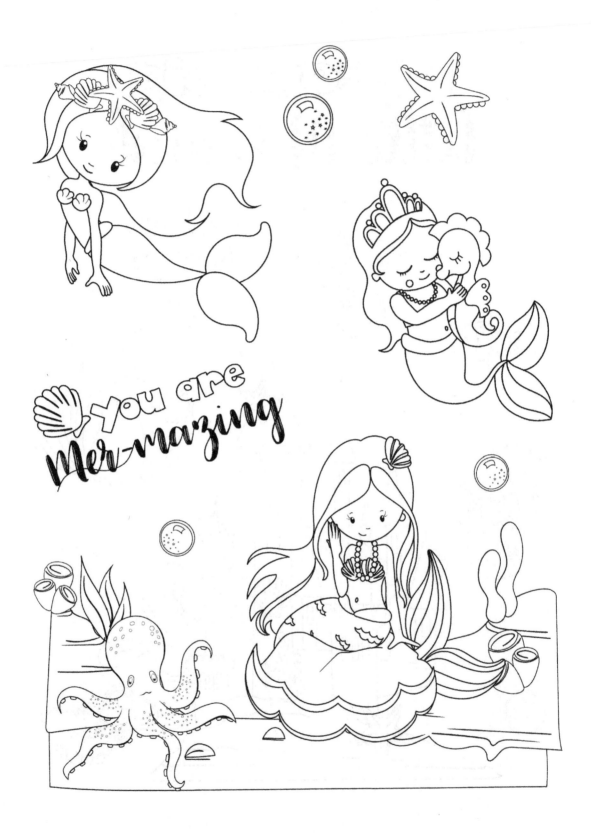

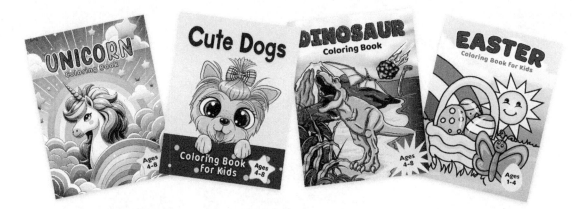

CHECK US OUT!

SAVE 20% OFF YOUR NEXT PURCHASE
ON OUR WEBSITE WITH THIS CODE:

THANKYOU20

WWW.GOLDENAGEPRESS.COM

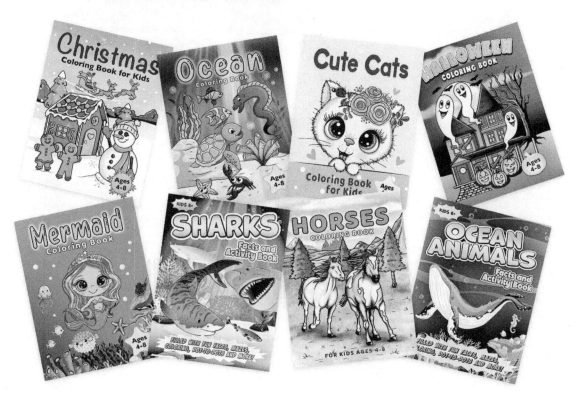

Made in the USA
Las Vegas, NV
06 December 2024